To My Honey.
Thanks

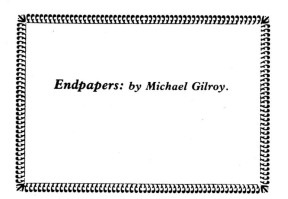

Endpapers: by Michael Gilroy.

A Beginner's Guide To
Lovebirds

Written By
Anmarie Barrie

Contents

© 1986 by T.F.H. Publications, Inc. Distributed in the UNITED STATES by T.F.H. Publications, Inc., 211 West Sylvania Avenue, Neptune City, NJ 07753; in CANADA by H & L Pet Supplies Inc., 27 Kingston Crescent, Kitchener, Ontario N2B 2T6; Rolf C. Hagen Ltd., 3225 Sartelon Street, Montreal 382 Quebec; in CANADA to the Book Trade by Macmillan of Canada (A Division of Canada Publishing Corporation), 164 Commander Boulevard, Agincourt, Ontario M1S 3C7; in ENGLAND by T.F.H. Publications Limited, 4 Kier Park, Ascot, Berkshire SL5 7DS; in AUSTRALIA AND THE SOUTH PACIFIC by T.F.H. (Australia) Pty. Ltd., Box 149, Brookvale 2100 N.S.W., Australia; in NEW ZEALAND by Ross Haines & Son, Ltd., 18 Monmouth Street, Grey Lynn, Auckland 2 New Zealand; in SINGAPORE AND MALAYSIA by MPH Distributors (S) Pte., Ltd., 601 Sims Drive, #03/07/21, Singapore 1438; in the PHILIPPINES by Bio-Research, 5 Lippay Street, San Lorenzo Village, Makati Rizal; in SOUTH AFRICA by Multipet Pty. Ltd., 30 Turners Avenue, Durban 4001. Published by T.F.H. Publications, Inc. Manufactured in the United States of America by T.F.H. Publications, Inc. © 1986 by T.F.H. Publications, Inc. Ltd.

1.
Introduction

Lovebirds are brightly colored, short tailed birds from 4½ to 7 inches long. They are naturally found in the tropical parts of Africa and on the island of Madagascar. Their range includes open land, wooded areas, forests and cultivated land. They feed on grains, seeds, fruits,

Their beautiful brightness of coloration is one of the reasons why Lovebirds are as popular as they are. Photo Vogelpark Walsrode.

buds, and seeding grasses. Lovebirds usually nest in large flocks, and sometimes smaller groups will break off to roost. The birds spend much of their time perching closely and preening one another, but quarrels do occur. Even mated pairs are known to bicker and fight.

In the wild, Lovebirds are rather quiet and secretive. When raised in captivity, they are strong and aggressive birds, able to torment many birds even larger than themselves.

Classified as species of parrots, Lovebirds display the characteristics common to all parrots. They have hooked bills, a relatively large skull, a thick tongue adapted for grasping, special feathers called powder downs, and feet with two toes pointing forward and two facing backward.

Lovebirds are popular captive birds because of their small size, their hardiness, and their vivid colors. The basic color of all the species is green, ranging from strong, bright shades to delicate pastels. Almost all exhibit a face and head of contrasting color, or at least a colored bill. In fact, many of the popular names for the species are derived from the plumage of the face.

The life expectancy of Lovebirds is from 15 to 25 years.

Lovebirds as pets

When purchasing any pet, not only the good points but the disadvantages must be considered as well. A Lovebird can only thrive in a home to which it is well suited. Lovebirds are good ornamental pets because of their striking appearance, comical behavior, and expressive personalities. Pretty birds, they are best kept in pairs to bring out their charm and liveliness.

Though the birds spend a lot of time perching together and preening one another, they are quarrelsome by nature. Even mated pairs are known to have spats. Therefore, they need roomy living quarters, not only to allow flight, but to keep fighting to a minimum. Because of their spitefulness, they are best kept apart from other species of bird. They are able to intimidate even those birds larger than themselves!

Birds are ideal pets in homes that cannot accommodate other domesticated animals. No apartment is too small to house a Lovebird cage. However, some species of Lovebirds do not adapt well to confinement and must be kept in aviaries. These types flourish only in large, outdoor aviaries, and fortunately they are hardy animals, able to survive the winters in temperate zones. Consideration must be given to those people living nearby, though, because some of these birds are noisy neighbors having loud and shrill voices.

Other parrots are more easily bred than Lovebirds, but the Lovebirds' small size, cleanliness, hardiness, and ease of care make them ideal pets. They are a long-lasting source of entertainment, but because they can be kept safely out of the way, they pose no threat to children, strangers, or other animals.

Lovebirds are readily available in many pet shops, and the rarity of the species will determine the price. No Lovebird should be purchased with the expectation that it will talk, but most people think that a great personality is more endearing than speech. These birds are not easily tamed, but if you plan to make the attempt, one must be purchased at a very young age, between five and six weeks. Patience and persistence on the part of the trainer is necessary to bring about the desired results.

Younger Lovebirds are easier to train than older individuals. Photo by Michael Gilroy.

Lovebirds require little maintenance, and the subsequent expenses are minimal. Food and water need to be freshened daily, and the cage and accessories need routine cleaning. Their diet is a simple one, and readily available all year 'round. All birds are sensitive to abrupt changes in their diet and susceptible to drafts and chills.

Lovebirds can be left alone for a couple of days with the proper provisions, but if a more extended trip is planned, then a reliable person needs to visit the birds every day to replenish the food and water. Of course, a Lovebird's cage is easily transported to another location to receive care. Just be sure to shield the bird from sudden temperature changes and drafts.

If you allow the bird to have free flying liberties in the home, remember that there is no record of a Lovebird being housebroken!

2.
Selection

Most importantly, buy a healthy bird. A sick bird demands more fuss and attention.

A variety of stores and breeders sell Lovebirds as pets. Seek out reputable enthusiasts who can offer sound ad-

Alertness and brightness of eye are two of the key points to check in determining whether a Lovebird is healthy; don't buy a listless bird. Photo by Michael Gilroy.

vice, for these are the people to refer to when you need help. Choose a breeder with a long-standing record of good stock. He won't sell a poor specimen that may mar his high standing. If purchasing from a store, choose one with clean, neat cages and well stocked inventories. These shops care for their birds and will probably have all the accessories you need to equip your bird. If the birds are well-fed and well-housed, they are more likely to be healthy specimens.

Look for a Lovebird that is active and alert. It should be bright-eyed and have an inquisitive disposition. Stand back from the cage to avoid interfering with the bird's natural antics, and observe its behavior for as long as possible. Note any extended periods of lethargy or uneasiness. The bird should be socializing with its cagemates and taking an active interest in its food.

The Lovebird should have a sleek, well-groomed appearance. The plumage should be full and healthy, with no bare spots on the body. A puffed up and tired look can mean that the bird is sleepy, but it can also indicate illness. A healthy Lovebird will sleep on one leg, whereas an ill bird will remain on two because of its weakened condition. The feet should have a firm, even grip.

If possible, handle the bird in the store. Thoroughly examine it. The breast should be full, plump, and firm, with no protruding bone. Avoid a bird with watery eyes and nostrils, or with sores or wounds anywhere on the body. The feathers should be smooth and clean, not broken or dirty. A soiled or pasty vent indicates diarrhea. Look at the droppings on the cage bottom. They should be small, firm (not hard), and dark in color, with a bit of white matter in them. Loose, watery droppings, or those of an unusual color, signal disease.

The mandibles should come together nicely and not be deformed or overgrown. The breathing should be slow and even, not labored or irregular.

If you plan to tame the bird, it must be young. Select a bird with black markings on the bill. This black is not present in mature birds. Young birds can be tamed by a persistent trainer with a good technique, but older birds are rather unyielding and spiteful. Babies between five and six weeks old are the best choice. They are totally independent of their parents, yet young enough to adapt to environmental changes. If you are lucky enough to find hand-reared chicks, they are more easily tamed because they are accustomed to human handling.

For taming purposes, buy only one bird. Additional birds will be more interested in each other than the trainer. If you do not intend to tame a Lovebird, then certainly buy two so their natural pairing behavior can be fully appreciated. Even Lovebirds of the same sex can be housed together as a pair. Females are likelier to be more compatible than males. Keeping two birds of the same sex prevents the couple from surprising you by breeding unexpectedly. Some female pairs have been known to lay eggs, although they are of course infertile.

If you are buying birds for immediate breeding, they should be no less than one year of age. Some breeders prefer to wait until the birds are in their second year.

Bringing the Lovebird home

Birds are typically placed in boxes so that you can bring them home with ease. Having the cage and all its accessories prepared in advance lessens the time your Lovebird has to spend in the box.

Since birds are susceptible to drafts and chills, keep the Lovebirds warm during transport. The journey itself will be trauma enough, so if possible avoid any additional shock. Moving the animals on a cold, windy, or damp day increases the chance of their becoming ill.

You may hesitate to handle the birds if you lack previous experience. Lovebirds do bite, so you may like to wear a pair of thin cotton gloves when grasping a bird. Or you may wrap your fingertips with adhesive strips or tape. Bulky gloves, or those that are brightly colored, may frighten a bird even more.

Use a firm but gentle touch when taking a bird out of the box and putting it in the cage. Always support the full weight of its body; do not grab it by the throat, feet, or tail. If a bird does happen to fly free, simply retrieve it with a net, light towel or cloth. Another approach is to line up the cage door with the opening of the box. Hold the box steady and allow the bird to hop out of the box and into the cage.

You may want to take the birds to a veterinarian before bringing them home. Make an arrangement with the shopkeeper for a refund or exchange if the vet declares them unfit.

If you presently have other birds at home, be sure to quarantine all new birds for 30 to 60 days before introducing them to the flock. Some illnesses are not immediately detectable and may be passed along to other animals.

3.
Housing

Housing that is too cramped results in the birds growing dull and losing their characteristic lively behavior. Indoor or outdoor aviaries are the prime choice. They afford the most flight room for your pet. Lovebirds can remain outside the year 'round in temperate zones as

Your pet shop will have a wide selection of modern, scientifically designed cages, and your pet dealer will be able to help you in making your selection. Photo by Dr. Herbert R. Axelrod.

long as they have a frost-free shelter to protect them from the elements. Commercially designed aviaries can be bought, or you can construct one yourself from metal or wood covered with wire mesh. Remember that Lovebirds like to chew and gnaw, so anything made of wood needs to be protected, or it will soon be destroyed. The wire mesh needs to be buried two to three feet in the soil to keep out predatory animals that will burrow under the aviary walls. Animals such as rats, mice, and the like will not only eat the food you set out for your bird, but may attack the Lovebirds themselves.

Position the aviary so that a section of it is always shaded. Then your pets can protect themselves from becoming overheated. Provide one nest box for each pair, plus some additional boxes to minimize fights over roosting sites. Be selective of what plants and shrubs you place within the aviary. All of them will be chewed by the Lovebirds so avoid those that are poisonous to your pets.

Ideally, the floor should be made of cement. Dirt floors can be saturated with droppings and may become contaminated. Cement floors are easier to clean and last longer than other types, but of course they are initially more expensive. Do not feed the Lovebirds by scattering the food on the floor where it can be fouled by droppings. Place it in dishes or on shelves where the birds can peck at it.

The doors of the aviary should be less than the full height of the flight. Birds fly up when they are nervous or excited, so they will fly to the ceiling of the aviary rather than out a door.

An alternative is to equip the aviary with double doors. As you enter the first door, there should be enough

Don't choose too small a cage; a roomy cage is a good investment.

space for you to close it before opening the second door. Any bird that manages to exit the interior door is trapped in the little anteroom.

Of course, most Lovebirds will be kept in cages within the home. Choose the largest cage you can comfortably accommodate and best afford. The minimum should be 20 inches square and 20 inches high. A cage that is too confining limits the birds' activity and the feathers constantly rub against the walls and become frayed. The larger the cage, the more freedom of flight. Exercise is essential in maintaining a healthy bird.

Select a metal cage with vertical wires close enough together to prevent a Lovebird from entrapping its head. Horizontal wires not only act as reinforcement for a strong cage, but provide a foothold for a bird as it climbs up and down the sides of the cage. And because these birds chew, a wooden cage would soon need to be replaced.

Some owners prefer a box cage for their Lovebirds. Three sides and the top are closed by metal or wood, much like a cabinet, and the front is made of metal bars, glass or transparent plastic. These enthusiasts believe that type of cage gives their birds a better sense of security. It also greatly reduces a Lovebird's exposure to drafts. This cage blocks a lot of light and therefore needs a light source. A fluorescent bulb, 15 to 20 watts, can be installed on/from the ceiling. A standard bulb throws off too much heat.

Deciding where in the house to place the cage is an important consideration. Avoid kitchens where drastic temperature changes are common. Heaters and radiators can be drying, and thereby damaging to the feathers. The room should be free of smoke and well ventilated, the cage placed away from drafty windows and doors. Captive birds have a thinner coat of down and so are more susceptible to chills. An area of indirect natural light is preferred because prolonged exposure to sunlight can overheat a bird.

To fully appreciate a Lovebird's antics, place the cage at eye level. Supporting it on a stand or hanging it from the ceiling are both acceptable. Do not place the cage on the floor because being so low may make the birds uncomfortable. In the wild, danger (predatory birds) comes from above. Setting the cage against a wall or in a corner increases the sense of security because the bird is not exposed on all sides. This is much the same idea as having a box cage, but a box cage is usually not as attractive as a wire cage.

Many cages come with food and water dishes that can be hung from the sides of the cage. This avoids tipping and lessens the chance of droppings contaminating the contents. There may also be individual doors to each dish, making access easy for cleaning and refilling. If a cage does not have containers, or you find that you need extra ones, they can be bought. Some can be hooked to the cage walls; others are simply placed on the floor. Do not put these dishes directly under a perch or they will be quickly soiled with droppings.

Lovebirds feed by cracking open seeds, eating the meat, and dropping the hull back into the dish. These hulls accumulate on top of the remaining seed and need to be removed periodically throughout the day or some birds won't find the rest of the food underneath them. You

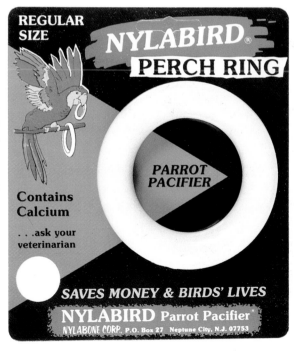

Your pet dealer should have a wide selection of accessories and bird toys; make sure that any toy you use is safe, such as the Nylabird perch ring shown here.

may like to use seed hoppers instead of open dishes. Seed hoppers have drawers that catch the hulls, then can be removed and emptied. The seed, though, is partially hidden by this drawer, and some birds may have trouble locating it. Be sure your pet knows where to find its food if a seed hopper is used.

Place several perches of varying diameters in the cage. Having them in different sizes exercises the feet and legs because of the changing footholds. Do not put the perches over food and water dishes, and position them so the Lovebirds have plenty of head clearance. Leave enough room between the perch and the wall so the tail and wing feathers do not rub against the wall and become damaged.

Do not crowd your birds with accessory items. Simple toys and gadgets can be clipped to the cage for amusement. A Lovebird will spend many hours before a mirror chattering to itself. Be inventive. A branch from a tree that can be chewed and stripped is great fun. Play stands can be purchased or made. Include a ladder, a swing, a bell, and other games. Be sure that all materials are non-toxic, have no sharp edges, and no small pieces can be broken off and swallowed.

Line the cage bottom with a paper or plastic lining. Do not use newspaper because the ink will rub off and dirty a Lovebird's feathers. On top of this, spread a layer of corn cob or wood shavings for extra absorbency. Sawdust scatters easily as the birds flutter and it may also stick to their wings. Do not use sand or gravel paper unless the cage has a bottom grate. This grate prevents the bird from eating soiled sand and fallen food and becoming ill. It also keeps the bird from walking in its own droppings. Be sure that the wiring of the grate is not a size that will trap a bird's feet or head. Some cages come with a sliding tray floor to facilitate cleaning. In others, the wire top is detachable and can be placed on a floor or mat while the litter is replaced. Every two or three days, dispose of the old contents and replace it with a fresh lining and bedding.

Wash and dry the cage bottom weekly, and periodically wipe the cage bars. Scrubbing with a stiff brush will loosen any dried debris. Clean the perches with a brush, fine sandpaper, or a perch scraper. Before putting them back into the cage, allow them to dry completely. Wet and dirty perches can cause arthritis, rheumatism, and colds. Every day wash the food and water dishes with hot soap and water. Dry them thoroughly because any remaining moisture will spur the growth of mold.

All animals need their rest to remain in top condition. In the wild, Lovebirds experience a twelve hour day. At night, they should be allowed twelve hours of undisturbed sleep. If their room is not quiet and dark, a drape or cloth placed over the cage will do as well. This cloth can also serve to calm the birds should they become noisy or anxious. Once quieted, the covering should be removed.

Of course, some owners have unusual schedules and prefer to have their birds awake when they are home. Lovebirds can adjust to such a routine as long as they have other times to nap throughout the day.

If you would like to bring your caged pets outside, hang the cage high in a tree, out of direct sunlight and out of reach of curious animals and children. It is safe to leave the cage on the ground only if the area is free of danger and you are in constant supervision. Remember that your Lovebirds are helpless prey and cannot flee from any harm that may present itself.

Bathing

A bowl or dish, with a heavy base to prevent tipping, can be placed in the cage as a bath. Your Lovebird can splash about to its heart's content, and may even emerge dripping wet. At first the bird may be a little hesitant, so splash it with some water to give it the general idea. Bathing keeps the feathers clean and the colors bright.

Because bathing can be rather a wet and messy business, special bathing dishes are available. The bird enters an enclosed dish and splashes about, while the surrounding area remains relatively dry. With a regular bowl or dish, the cage bedding needs to be replaced and the bars wiped dry.

Some birds never take a liking to bathing. Do not force them. An alternative is to squirt them with warm water from a spray bottle.

The preferred bath time is early in the day. This allows a bird plenty of time for drying out before the lower nighttime temperatures set in. While the bird is damp, it is even more crucial to protect it from drafts and chills.

During warm weather, giving the bird a bath or a spraying is a good way to keep it cool. As the weather turns colder, showers and baths should be given only on warm and sunny days.

Lovebirds with extended flying liberties can even bathe in a sink and be squirted with a sprayer. Some birds enjoy this so much that they fly to the sink when they hear the sound of running water! Moisture is particularly important during incubation of the eggs.

4.
Nutrition

A balanced diet, clean living conditions, and plenty of exercise circumvent many diseases and breeding disorders. Should your pet become ill, a disease will have a more ravaging effect on a poorly nourished body. Since no one food provides all the essential nutrients for

A good basic diet enriched properly with vitamin and mineral supplements will go a long way towards keeping your bird healthy.

growth and maintenance, a variety of seeds, greens, and animal proteins needs to be offered as a guard against malnutrition and deficiencies. Seed mixtures supply most of the protein, fats, and carbohydrates necessary for a Lovebird's survival. Fruits, vegetables, and greens are a good source of roughage, fiber, and a large number of vitamins and minerals.

Protein is essential for the formation and maintenance of body tissues.prime sources of it are fish, milk, buttermilk, cheese, eggs and peanut butter. It aids in the production of keratin, used in the formation of the beak, feathers, and claws.

Too little fat results in dry skin and feathers. Necessary for the proper absorption of some vitamins, fats also help to heat, insulate, and protect against injury. Seeds, fish oils, and eggs are good sources of fat.

Seeds, cereal grains, and fruit contain carbohydrates, and the roughage they provide aids in digestion.

Vitamin A is required for the normal development of bone structure and in building immunity against disease. It also contributes to proper growth, good vision, and maintenance of healthy skin and mucous membranes. Foods rich in vitamin A include apples, carrots, corn, fish, eggs, milk, and milk products. Greens like dandelions, celery, spinach, and lettuce, as well as fruits like bananas and tomatoes, are high in vitamin A.

The vitamins in the B complex are important for growth and hatchability. Vitamin B is crucial to the metabolism of fats and carbohydrates, and for the maintenance of the nervous system. The best sources of vitamin B are yeast, wheat germ, and whole wheat bread.

Found especially in citrus fruits, vitamin C is involved in the production of connective tissue.

Important in the production of keratin, vitamin D is also critical during breeding for the formation of eggshells. It is involved in the production of bone and is responsible for regulating the balance of certain minerals. Eggs and fish oils are also good suppliers of vitamin D.

Other vitamins, as well as minerals and elements, are just as vital to a healthy bird. A lack of any one of them can cause severe problems, which is why a rich and varied diet is crucial.

The basic food for Lovebirds is a mixture of dried seeds consisting of canary seed, millet, sunflower, oats, and hemp. Commercially prepared parakeet food provides these seeds and others. Make sure this basic mixture is always available. Your bird's digestive system will extract almost every nutrient available, and yet there is no danger of a bird eating too much and getting fat as a result. About two thirds of the diet should be seeds and one third fruits, vegetables, and other foods.

Lettuce, spinach, watercress and carrot and celery tops are all popular greens with Lovebirds. Local weeds and grasses like chickweed, leaf buds, and dandelion leaves are also a good source. Be sure to wash the greens thoroughly to remove dirt and traces of insecticides which may be toxic to your pet. You may be able to work out an arrangement with your local grocer to regularly pick up his produce scraps. Greens can be clipped to the cage wires with a clothespin. Do not offer your bird any food that is not as fresh as what you yourself would eat. Wilted foods are dangerous. Fortunately, a Lovebird is not likely to eat something that is not good for it.

Almost all kinds of fruit are eaten by Lovebirds. Figs, berries, apples, bananas, pears, grapes or anything else can be offered. Pieces of fruit can be pushed between the bars of the cage for your bird to peck at. It is best to provide fruits and vegetables in the morning and then remove them before they turn bad. Do not leave them overnight because they may spoil by morning.

Introduce new foods gradually, and not too many at one time because a Lovebird's system can be upset by changes. Even though your bird may not seem interested in new foods, always offer it a variety. Allow the bird to develop its own tastes.

Freshly washed branches (including leaves) of poplar, maple, willow, fruit trees and others provide good nutrition and are chewed lustily. They satisfy the gnawing instinct. The bark is rich in minerals and trace elements. Other treats include spray millet, seed bells and egg biscuits used for parakeets.

Even though Lovebirds get much of their moisture from fresh, juicy greens, clean drinking water should always be present. Once or twice a week the water can be fortified with a liquid vitamin supplement. A few drops of cod liver oil or wheat germ oil can be added to the seed periodically, especially during breeding. Keep this seed in a dish separate from the regular because it is fattening and the oil causes the seed to spoil more quickly.

No more than a three to four weeks supply of seed should be kept on hand in order to avoid spoilage. Over a period of time, the seed can dry out and lose its nutritional value. Seal it in moisture-proof containers in a cool, dry place. Moisture and humidity foster molds that will make a bird ill.

Cuttlebone is inexpensive and easy to use, so obtain a supply for your Lovebirds. Photo by Vincent Serbin.

There are two tests to determine the nutritional value of the seed. First, the seed should taste sweet and nutty, not sour or bitter. Second, wet the seed and place it on a damp paper towel or in some dirt. Keep it moist and in a few days it should sprout. If it does not, then it has no value as hard seed either. The sprouts are especially high in protein and can be fed to your bird. Seed soaked in water for 24 hours is also a good dietary supplement. The soaked seed undergoes the same chemical processes as germinated seed and so provides valuable nutrients.

If you follow this routine, there will be no need for special foods, tonics, or conditioners because a properly cared for bird will be healthy. A poor diet and improper living conditions may lead to illness. After your bird has settled in and developed a routine, monitor its food intake over a week. Take note of how much and what types of food it consumes. In the future, you will be able to assess any changes indicating disease or injury. When molting or during cold weather, a bird may eat more in an effort to maintain its body temperature.

Grit and Cuttlebone

Grit is stored in the gizzard as an aid in the digestion of husked seed. The grinding action has the same function as teeth in other animals. Grit also contains essential minerals and elements for your pet. Ideally, charcoal and some other organic material, like oyster shells or barnacles, should be mixed with the grit. Some grit, or bird sand, contain these compounds, others do not. These additives can be purchased separately and added by you. Dried, crushed eggshells are an acceptable substitute. These organic supplements are especially important during breeding. Keep the grit mixture in a dish apart from the regular seed, and replace it weekly.

Cuttlebone is the internal shell of the cuttlefish, a marine animal closely related to the octopus and squid. Mostly calcium carbonate, this substance is utilized for egg-shell production, bone building, feather growth, a strong beak and helps to prevent egg binding. During breeding, the consumption of cuttlebone may be doubled. Gnawing on the cuttlebone, a similar mineral block, or a Nylabird pacifier helps to keep the beak trim and satisfy the chewing need.

Cuttlebone usually comes with a clip for attaching it to the cage. If it has none, simply punch holes in it and fasten it with wire near a perch.

5.
Taming

Despite their name, Lovebirds are not one of the friendliest or easiest species of parrot to tame. Young birds, around five or six weeks of age, are most desirable for taming. These birds are just out of the nest and independent of their parents. Their bite is not as severe as

Lovebirds, unfortunately, don't always get along as well together as the pair shown here; they can be very quarrelsome. Photo by Louise van der Meid.

that of a mature bird. A Lovebird that does not show any black markings on the bill is already at least two months old and will be more difficult to tame. As with any bird, though, the more time invested, the faster the desired results. Develop a regular training routine and stick to it for several weeks. Don't be slack and then blame lack of success on the bird's being "untamable."

Stick or hand taming inside the cage is not necessary with Lovebirds. You will probably be bitten more with this approach than by proceeding directly to taming out of the cage. Even if you tame the bird to rest on your hand in the cage, once you bring the Lovebird out it will try to get away from you.

The first step in taming is to clip the bird's wings. The bird won't be able to travel as far in its flight before having to land. Because Lovebirds are so small and light, though, you will be surprised by how well they can maneuver even with their wings clipped.

The taming area should be a small room, like a bathroom. The bird won't have far to fly, and you won't have far to follow. The less furniture and high perches in the room make for fewer things for the bird to bump into or hide behind. This makes retrieval that much easier. Make sure there is no escape through an open door or window. Close the drapes so the bird won't fly into a window; cover all mirrors. If there is no carpeting, spread out a towel or other padding to cushion any falls and to provide traction.

If you are intimidated by the Lovebird's bite, cover your fingers with adhesive strips or tape. A snug pair of cotton or thin leather gloves will also give some protection; bulky gloves, or those not of a neutral color, may upset a bird. If the bird does bite, gently press your fingers into the corners of its mandibles to make it release its hold.

Choose a family member with plenty of time and motivation to do the initial taming. Throughout the day give short lessons (fifteen to twenty minutes) to keep the bird from overtiring and losing interest. If too much time passes between lessons, continuity is lost. Each time the bird is removed from the cage give it a taming lesson. The more accustomed a bird is to human handling, the easier it will be to tame.

The fewer accessories and activities there are in the room, the less distraction there is for the pet. Having only the trainer in the room is less confusing for both the bird and the instructor.

Scatter a few seeds in front of the cage to entice the bird to come out. If it won't venture out on its own, then retrieve it with a stick or your hand. Always speak and whistle softly to the bird to keep it calm. Avoid any sudden or jerking movements that may excite and frighten it.

Work close to the floor by getting on your knees. This shortens any falls the Lovebird might experience during a session.

Move slowly, approaching the Lovebird from the front. Do not sneak up on it from behind and grab it. A frightened bird is not trainable. Of course a bird will initially avoid your advances, but by not alarming it, it will relax and realize no harm is intended.

Gently push a dowel or stick against the bird's chest to get it to climb up. The Lovebird may try to run or fly, so backing it into a corner may make this easier to ac-

This Lovebird has been taught how to move from the stick onto the finger of its owner. Photo by Risa Teitler.

complish. Do not chase it around, but let the bird come to a rest and then approach it. Teach it to step on and off the stick, either onto the floor or onto another stick. Twisting the stick with a rolling motion causes the bird to step forward and off the dowel. If your pet is a biter, it will grab and gnaw the stick instead of your hand. Having the Lovebird stick-tamed comes in handy when you need to retrieve it from high places.

Once the bird is accustomed to the stick, have it step onto your hand. Pass it back and forth between your hand and the stick, then from hand to hand. Repetition is the key to success.

Sometimes a bird will use its beak to steady itself when climbing. This is not intended as a bite.

Let the bird perch on your hand until it is calm, then

slowly stand up. This may need to be repeated several times before the bird remains in place. Now you can coax it onto your shoulder. With a rolling motion of your hand, the bird will be forced to step on your shoulder to regain its balance. Just remember, there is no such thing as a housebroken Lovebird!

Reward good behavior with stroking, praise, and food. Ignore anything else. It may take a little while for your bird to accept food from your hand. Be patient. For a particularly stubborn bird, remove all food from its cage an hour before a taming session. The bird may be more likely to eat what you offer. Of course, do not deny your bird any provisions for an extended period, and do not use this technique as punishment. After a session, no matter what the result, give it plenty of food and water. It will probably be tired and thirsty.

Train the Lovebird for longer periods each day. Once tame, introduce other family members to it to avoid a one-person bird. Have them feed and play with it.

The least you should expect from taming is to have the Lovebird rest comfortably on your hand. With the bird feeling safe and secure in your hands, it will be easier to examine and treat it in the future.

If you allow your bird free-flying periods, put aside all items worth saving that can be chewed. Lovebirds are curious, active birds that are inclined to investigate and get into mischief. Always supervise the bird to prevent the gnawing of furniture, plants and papers. Chew toys are a good diversion. Nylabird® products are available at your local pet shop and are excellent for this purpose. Feeding a Lovebird only in its cage will train it to return there when hungry or thirsty. A dish filled with fresh food can be very enticing.

Utilize a Lovebird's natural antics to teach it some simple tricks. It can play tug-of-war, climb ladders, ring bells, and place items in a cup. Behavior like spreading its wings on command can be reinforced. Think of advanced training as an extension of the initial taming. Again, repetition and reward work best. Practice one activity until it is mastered, then introduce another. Do not confuse your bird with too many things at once.

Wing clipping

Done correctly, wing clipping is quick, easy and painless for your bird. Clipping the wing feathers simply means that the bird can fly only a short distance before losing its balance and having to land. During taming, a clipped bird requires less chasing. The sessions are also less tiring for both you and the Lovebird. Should a clipped bird happen to find its way outdoors, you can retrieve it with a little effort. However, an unclipped bird is probably lost forever.

Clipping only one wing results in the bird's losing control over its flight direction. A bird that cannot fly where it intends to is more quickly discouraged and readily tamed. Because Lovebirds are so small and light, that one wing needs to be clipped extensively and properly. Even so, the bird will be able to maneuver surprisingly well.

It is a good idea to have the Lovebird's wing clipped by an experienced bird handler, such as a dealer or an avian veterinarian. This prevents the bird from associating a bad experience with its new home or owner. It also gives you the opportunity to observe the procedure should you decide to do it yourself in the future.

Two people should work together to do the clipping; one holds the bird while the other clips. The bird should be held so that its head is between the fore and middle fingers. Keep the head straight without pushing or pulling the neck. The ring finger and pinkie support the back, while the thumb acts as a perch for the feet. Monitor the bird's respiration and note any distress.

Extend both wings and examine the feathers. Choose the wing that has no blood feathers. These are new feathers growing in that still have a blood vein in the quill. They must not be cut or bleeding will occur. If both wings have blood feathers, select the wing with the fewest and simply clip around the blood feathers. If you do happen to clip one, apply styptic powder to stop the bleeding.

With a pair of small wire cutters or barber's scissors, cut along the tips of the covert feathers. Leave as they are one or two feathers next to the bird's torso and the first two feathers on the end of the wing. Trim no closer than three-quarters of an inch of the quill emerging from the wing.

If you plan to keep the bird clipped, check for new growth periodically. The flight feathers will be fully re-grown in about six months.

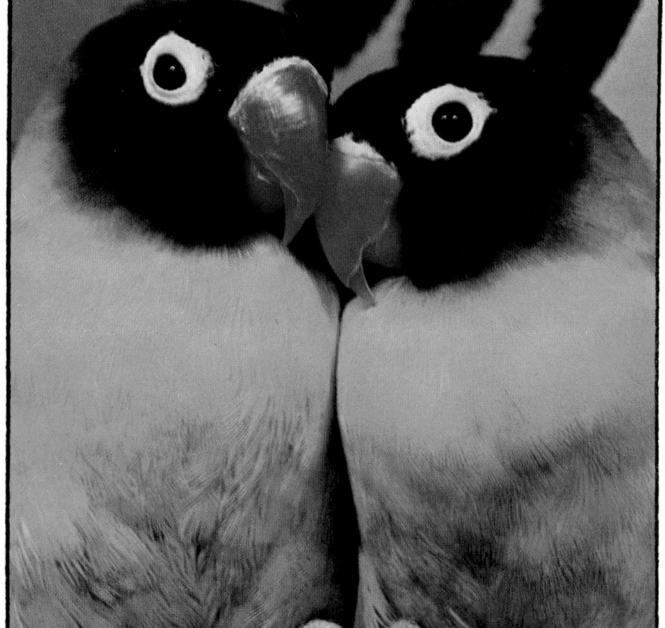

6.
Ailments

Lovebirds are hardy animals if not exposed to unfavorable conditions. Stressful situations, like abrupt temperature changes, malnutrition, disease and filth all pose a danger to health. If treated with thought and care, Lovebirds will thrive in captivity. Preventive mainte-

Regardless of which of the generally available Lovebird species you have (Masked Lovebirds, Agapornis personata, *shown on facing page; Fischer's Lovebird,* Agapornis fischeri, *shown above) your bird will be a healthy, long-lived creature if you provide it with good basic care.*

Lovebirds preen one another with their beaks, but the beaks also can cause wounds when used as weapons—as they sometimes are. Photo by Dr. Herbert R. Axelrod.

nance is the most important aspect. Of course, accidents and illness can happen, but do not panic. Simple problems can be remedied with immediate and proper attention. For something more serious, consult a veterinarian.

Many symptoms indicate that a Lovebird is ill. Note any change in the bird's general appearance or habits. An absence of activity and ruffled feathers are an attempt to conserve body heat. (An ill bird has difficulty maintaining body temperature.)

Any discharge from the eyes or nose or any change in the droppings indicate a disease. Take note of the amount of food consumed. Either an increase or decrease may be noteworthy.

Isolate sick birds, away from all others, in a hospital cage. One can be bought, rented or made by yourself. Simply cover all but the front of the regular cage, or a smaller one, with plastic or cloth to block drafts and outside stimulation that may excite the bird. Suspend a light bulb, or place the cage on a heating pad for additional warmth. A temperature of 90 degrees should be constantly maintained.

Remove all perches and toys and place the food and water dishes on the floor. Your pet may become very fussy about the food that it eats, so provide some of its favorites. A balanced diet is still preferred, but getting the bird to eat something is more important.

Use a towel or glove to transfer an untamed Lovebird. If the bird is tame, these precautions are unnecessary.

If you need to transport the bird to a vet, keep it warm and quiet. Avoid drastic temperature changes.

Examining the breast of a male Pied Peach-faced Lovebird. Photo by Louise van der Meid.

Molting

Throughout the year, the feathers are constantly being replaced. If the bird begins to lose an unusual amount of feathers, it may be the result of overheating or a dietary imbalance. Remove the bird from drying heat sources and check the diet. Seeds rich in oils, and fish oils periodically added to the food, help to keep the skin and feathers in good condition. Baths and showers are also recommended.

Cuts
Sterilize wounds with hydrogen peroxide on a cotton ball or swab. Apply a little pressure to help stop bleeding. Styptic powder can also be used.

A bird's general deportment tells a good deal about its state of health, and changes in its behavior are especially significant. Photo by Vincent Serbin.

Feather plucking

In this condition, the bird picks at its own feathers, resulting in damaged feathers and bald spots. Possible causes are anxiety, boredom, overbreeding or a diet lacking in mineral content. Act accordingly.

Conjunctivitis

The eyes will have a watery discharge, and your Lovebird will shut its eyes often and blink a lot. If the condition worsens daily, see a veterinarian for some medication.

Eye sores

Sores on the white eye ring can be a disease in itself, or a symptom of another infection or injury. This should be looked at by a veterinarian.

Egg binding

The hen may have labored breathing and an unhappy look about her because she is having difficulty passing an egg. The egg shell is soft due to poor nutrition, lack of exercise, or a young or overweight hen.

Do not attempt to expel the egg yourself because if it ruptures within the female she will die. Apply two to three drops of mineral oil to the vent and place her over a heat source, like a warm heating pad. Call a veterinarian for further instructions.

Internal parasites

This is a rare condition for Lovebirds. If you notice that your bird eats a lot yet is losing weight, bring a fresh stool sample to your veterinarian. A diagnosis can be made and proper medication prescribed.

The parasites are passed in the droppings, so be sure your bird does not ingest soiled food or water that may reintroduce them into its system.

Shock, concussion

Usually resulting from an injury, the bird lies still and may make some crying sounds. The breathing is shallow and the eyes do not focus. Do not handle the bird after moving it to a warm, protected spot. Minimize distur-

Lovebirds maintained under community conditions must be watched especially carefully to prevent outbreaks of communicable diseases. Photo by Glen S. Axelrod.

When holding a Lovebird for examination, make sure that you don't grip it too tightly. Photo by Vincent Serbin.

bances and put food and water within its reach. It may take some time for the bird to respond. Check it for other injuries that may need attention.

Dead in the shell

This is a common occurrence with Lovebirds where the chicks die in the eggshell before being hatched. It is caused by low humidity in the nest or a deficiency in the hen's diet. Keep the humidity high during incubation and provide bath water daily so that the damp feathers of the parents keep the shells moist.

Broken bones

Do not attempt to treat broken bones yourself because the injury may be more serious than it appears. If improperly splinted and bandaged, a broken leg may not heal properly and may leave the bird permanently crippled and unable to breed. The best advice is to see a veterinarian. It will take several weeks for the injury to heal.

Going light

The bird exhibits a marked weight loss. Sometimes associated with another illness, sometimes the cause is unknown. Provide more fattening food like oats, sunflower seeds, milk-soaked bread and corn kernels. Contact a veterinarian who may recommend an appetite stimulant.

Lice, mice, ticks

If your bird scratches a lot and bites continuously at its feathers, examine it for external parasites. These creatures feed on the skin, feathers, and blood of your pet.

Disinfect the cage and all the accessories immediately. Scrub everything with a stiff brush and use commercial preparations available on the market. A veterinarian will prescribe a suitable treatment for the bird.

Scaly legs, scaly face

This condition results from a mite that attacks all areas not covered by feathers. It starts on the cere and beak, then is spread to the eyes, vent and legs by scratching. Preparations for treatment must be applied in the early stages to be effective.

Heat stroke

Typically the result of a careless owner who left the bird exposed too long to direct or very strong reflected sunlight. Chances of recovery are slim if the condition is not detected soon enough. Spray or rub the bird with cool water until it responds.

Arthritis, rheumatism, leg cramps

Often caused by wet and dirty perches, perches that are too small in diameter for a proper grip, and confinement. Allow your bird plenty of space for movement and provide perches in varying diameters to exercise the feet and legs. Wash the perches regularly, and let them dry thoroughly before placing them back into the cage.

Overgrown beaks and claws

Having cuttlebone and other chew toys (Nylabird products) satisfy the gnawing instinct and help to keep the beak trim. If the beak does become overgrown, have it treated by a veterinarian. Overgrown claws are more common and easily remedied. Trim them with fingernail clippers a little at a time to avoid cutting a blood vessel. Treat with hydrogen peroxide and styptic powder if bleeding should occur. Smooth rough edges with a nail file. Natural wood perches help to keep the claws in good condition.

Constipation

Your Lovebird will have difficulty passing droppings which may be small and hard, or it may not be able to pass them at all. This is probably the result of an inferior diet, so increase the supply of fresh, green, leafy vegetable. For more severe cases your veterinarian may suggest a laxative.

Diarrhea

Diarrhea is usually a symptom of another ailment. The droppings are loose and watery and can vary in color. Sometimes there may be a foul odor. Weight loss and dehydration can be rapid because Lovebirds have such little body weight. Remove all fruits and vegetables until the stools firm up.

Diarrhea may also result from nervousness, an improper diet, or the consumption of unclean food or water.

Colds

Symptoms of a cold are lethargy, ruffled feathers, and runny eyes or nostrils. Sneezing, coughing, or wheezing may also be apparent.

Keep the bird warm and eliminate greens and juicy fruits. If the condition persists, consult a veterinarian. Not properly treated, a cold can lead to more serious and complicated respiratory infections.

7.
Breeding

A proper diet, a suitable nest, and a true pair are the essentials for breeding Lovebirds. Poor nutrition in the parents can result in egg binding, illness in the breeding pair, and infertile eggs. Parents may refuse, or be unable to take proper care of their young. If Lovebirds re-

Recently hatched Lovebirds and eggs in a nest box. Photo by L. van der Meid.

ceive only seeds during this time, the young will be small and weak, susceptible to disease, and have a shortened life span. The biggest problem encountered by breeders is finding a true male-female pair. At times, males may act like a pair and mate, and female couples have been known to lay and incubate infertile eggs. The best way to overcome this predicament is to buy a proven pair, or if you have an aviary, to buy several birds and allow them to choose a mate for themselves. Do not breed any Lovebirds before one year of age even though they may be sexually mature earlier. Some breeders prefer to wait until the birds are in their second year because the offspring of young birds may be small and weak, and the incidence of infertile eggs and dead-in-the-shell babies is higher.

A commercial parakeet nest box can be used for breeding Lovebirds, or you can construct one yourself. Fashion a wooden box (remember, Lovebirds like to chew) about 5 x 6 and 7 inches high. The top should be hinged for easy access and small ventilation holes placed high on the box. A hole two inches in diameter, large enough for the birds to enter but small enough to afford privacy, is placed about two inches from the top. This height prevents the chicks from venturing out at too young an age. A perch is attached just below the door to make entry easier. The nest box should be placed high in the cage or the aviary to make the birds feel more secure. If you are using a cage, the nest box should be attached outside it to maintain ample room inside. One or two cage wires can be cut and the entry of the nest box lined up to the space. When the nest box is removed, the hole can be patched with wire from a hanger or a piece of metal. To keep the adults from chewing the box, provide them with fresh twigs in the nest.

The preferred time for breeding is the spring. More seeding grasses and fresh vegetables are available, and the longer days mean more light hours to care for the young. Summer is often too hot, and cold weather increases the chances of birds getting chilled.

High humidity around 65% is vital for the development of the eggs. A vaporizer or a humidifier are good additions to the breeding, and every day the nest box, the nest, and the eggs can be sprayed with water to keep them moist. Nesting material like palm fronds, wood shavings, peat moss and bark should be placed in the cage for the female to carry into the nest box. She may even wet it in the bath or drinking water before carrying it off. Fresh water needs to be available every day for drinking, moistening the nesting material, and bathing. After the adults bathe, they will return to the nest and their damp feathers aid in keeping the humidity high. The moisture helps to soften the eggshells to ease the hatching.

After mating, the hen spends a lot of time in the nest box and the cock feeds her. She carries the nesting material to the box to make a nest and her droppings become larger. Five to six days after copulation, a lump appears at the base of her tail and she lays the first rounded, white egg. A clutch of four to five eggs will be laid, one every other day. After seven days of incubation, a fertile egg will show red veins, but an infertile egg will be opaque. After twenty one to twenty four days of incubation, the chicks will begin hatching in the same order as they were laid. For this entire period, the hen sits tight, leaving the nest only once or twice a day to feed, drink, bathe, and relieve herself.

If mating has not occurred in three or four weeks, illness may be suspected. Or, a simple change, like a new location or different bedding, can be tried. If all else fails, a new mate is the next choice. If mating took place but no eggs followed, a new hen is required. If eggs are laid but they were sterile, this is not uncommon. Sometimes the first one or two are not good, but from then on the chicks will develop. If it continues, a new cock is indicated.

The newly hatched chicks are blind, flesh colored, and covered with downy plumage. The color varies from whitish to red-orange depending on the species. In twelve days the babies can see, and soon after, pin feathers emerge. At around twenty one days the feathers begin to break through the shafts, and gradually the chicks are fully feathered.

The hen feeds her young by regurgitating food into their mouths. The male may help to join in with the feedings. By five to six weeks, the chicks venture outside the nest box and practice flying. At night they return to the nest box to sleep. After one more week, they no longer enter the nest box but remain sleeping in the cage. Their beaks may still be a bit soft, so offer them soaked seed. Place food and water dishes on the floor because they may not be able to find the adult dishes. By six to eight weeks the chicks are fully independent.

Illness, aggression, or abandonment may require you to hand-rear the chicks. Some breeders voluntarily remove the chicks two to three weeks after hatching because hand-fed Lovebirds are more docile, affectionate and less aggressive than birds that are tamed when young. The chicks are kept together for comfort and warmth, in a nest box. Initially they are fed four times daily from a small spoon or eye dropper. The feedings are reduced to two or three a day as they eat more and the crop remains full longer. Because the beaks are soft, they are not fed seed, but a commercially prepared nesting food or a homemade mixture of Pablum and baby food vegetables. The mixture should be moist and kept warm in a baby food server. Wipe the chicks clean with a damp cloth or cotton swab because any dried food on the body is irritating and can cause sores. As the beaks become firm, soaked seed and then hard seed can be introduced. When the chicks begin to feather, they can be transferred to a nursery cage.

While the young are still dependent on the parents, the pair may breed again. If you wish to interrupt the cycle, remove the nest box, discouraging further mating. No more than two clutches a season should be allowed because overbreeding is detrimental to the adults and their chicks.

Record keeping and banding

All birds captively bred should have good, clear records kept of matings. The information should include the bird's parents, its sex, date of birth, and its characteristics, both faults and attributes. Details should include breeding dates, date of eggs laid, number of hatchlings and their band numbers. Such records serve as guides when setting up pairs of birds. Healthy birds with good qualities will be bred, below average stock and birds with poor breeding records will be passed over, and overbreeding can be avoided.

Bands are useful tools for identification and controlled breeding, and they are a must for exhibition birds. A Lovebird cannot be shown without one. Some adult birds take offense to bands being placed on their young and will attempt to remove them. Fortunately, there are two types of rings that can be utilized.

The closed ring has to be placed on a young bird when it is a certain size. If the baby is too small, the ring will slip off. If the baby grows too large, the ring cannot be slipped over the foot. Grease the chick's foot with petroleum jelly or baby oil. Slide the ring over the forward toes and up the leg until it is past the rear toes. Wipe the feet clean with a soft, dry cloth. A plastic ring will soon be chewed off, so use only metal ones. These metal rings can be darkened in a flame and cooled. It may be their shininess that is so disturbing to the mother.

Open rings can be placed on a bird of any age or size. The ring is held by a special appliance that opens the band and then releases it when around the shank of the leg.

Rings can be bought in pet shops, or they can be ordered through your local bird club. Personalized bands with your name and address on them are available.

If you give your birds' offspring to a shopkeeper to be sold, the banding is the only way to identify your birds at a later date.

8.
Species

Although there are almost ten species of Lovebirds, most species are rarely offered for sale. In the United States and Great Britain, the three most commonly seen species are the Peach-faced Lovebird, Fischer's Lovebird, and the Masked Lovebird.

Agapornis lilianae, the Nyasa Lovebird, is relatively rarely seen. Photo by H. Reinhard.

Peach-faced Lovebird (*Agapornis roseicollis*)

Sometimes called the Rosy-faced Lovebird, the Peach-faced Lovebird is found mainly in Southwest Africa. The head is a bright rose, with the cheeks, throat and breast seeming pink or peach. The body of the bird is green, with a patch of blue on the rump. The tail and the wing feathers show some black barring. The bill is horn colored and the feet are gray. The males and females of the species show no sexual dimorphism.

The Peach-faced Lovebirds are rather spiteful, so it is not recommended to put a pair of them in with other birds. They are not only aggressive towards the other birds, but are also pugnacious towards each other. Even though the hens are dominant in nature, as a rule the hens get along better than cocks. If you plan to keep a pair without breeding them, choose females who are more likely to be peaceful. Of all the Lovebirds, the Peach-faced is one of the noisiest.

Of course, the Peach-faced Lovebirds have obviously been bred with much success because they are probably more numerous than all the other species of Lovebirds combined. The female carries nesting material by tucking it into the feathers of the lower back and rump. Even while the hen incubates the eggs, it is not unusual to observe both the hen and the cock roosting in the nest box.

Fischer's Lovebird (*Agapornis fischeri*)

Fischer's Lovebird comes from the Victoria Nyanza area of Africa. They are easily obtained but should be considered strictly an aviary bird. When confined to a cage, the Fischer's Lovebird display their unhappiness in a number of ways: they may molt continuously,

Abyssinian *Lovebird*, Agapornis taranta. *Photo by the San Diego Zoo.*

or hide their heads in a corner as though they have no interest in life, or they may become overweight which leads to a shortened life span.

The overall color of this species is green, with a patch of blue on the rump. The green tail feathers are tipped in blue also. The breast, neck and head are orange-red, the color being more distinct at the forehead and paling as it approaches the throat. The bill is red and the feet are gray-brown. The sexes are alike, but the species displays a white eye ring.

Red-faced Lovebird (*Agapornis pullaria*)

The Red-faced Lovebird is not one of the hardier species. When newly imported it requires a good deal of care. Exceptional pairs may live quite well in cages, but on the average, these birds do not take well to confinement. In an aviary with plenty of space, the constant activity of these birds is one of their greatest attractions.

This species is found mainly in central Africa. They are, on the whole, less colorful than most of the other Lovebirds, and the sexes do show some distinguishing characteristics. The body of the bird is green, with a blue rump and gray feet. The tail has a black band and red and green feathers. The bill is reddish-orange, and the top of the head and the forehead are bright, paling several shades on the cheeks and throat. Overall, the female is less intense, with the red actually tending towards orange. The red areas may be less in size than on the cock. The underwing coverts of the hen are green while in the cock they are usually black. In immature birds, the males have black wing coverts while the females lack this feature.

Male Madagascar Lovebird, Agapornis cana; *in this species it is easy to distinguish adult males from adult females. Photo by the San Diego Zoo.*

The Red-faced Lovebird is very difficult in captivity because in the wild they use termite mounds as nesting places.

Black-cheeked Lovebird *(Agapornis nigrigenis)*

Found in Zambia and the surrounding vicinity, the Black-cheeked Lovebird is presently rare, and so the price is comparatively high. This is unfortunate, since this species is probably the least spiteful, most friendly and best suited to cage life. With time, it will become reasonably tame, being much more manageable when handled by its owner. Breeders have also found this species not too difficult to breed, and the adults are good parents. The Black-cheeked Lovebirds are very hardy, capable of withstanding considerable variations in temperature.

The sexes of this species are the same, with green bodies and rose-colored bills. The forehead is brown, lightening on the crown, but darkening below the eyes. The cheeks and throat are very dark brown, though never absolutely black. On the throat is a distinctive salmon or reddish colored patch. This species has a white eye ring.

Black-masked Lovebird *(Agapornis personata)*

The Black-masked Lovebird, imported from the area around Tanzania, are extremely hardy birds, enduring temperatures around the freezing point with no harm. A pair can settle down to be quiet and peaceful birds, but these birds are not always well-tempered with other species, or even pairs of the same species.

Once a pair has decided to breed, they are inclined to do so all year 'round. Allowing birds to breed during the winter can result in egg-binding, and permitting any birds to mate continually will exhaust the parents. Both male and female help to build the nest, and this species is quite selective in the type of material they choose for this purpose.

The head color of the Black-masked Lovebirds is typically black but may vary to a dark brown. The neck and nape are a bright yellow, while the top of the back and the breast are of a paler shade. The back, wings, and tail feathers are green, while the underside is a yellow green. The rump is blue, and the tail feathers have black markings. The beak is red and the feet are brown. The species has a white eye ring.

Abyssinian Lovebird *(Agapornis taranta)*

At times referred to as the Black-winged Lovebird, the Abyssinian Lovebirds originate in the highlands of Ethiopia. They are slightly larger, a bit more thickset and not as attractive as the other species. They are hardy birds, but not considered free breeders or pleasant pets. Difficult to handle, this species never really becomes tame, pecking at other birds and anybody who attempts to handle them.

This species is varying shades of green all over but lacks any brightness or patch of color. On the male, across the forehead, is a red band, and around the eye are a number of red feathers not present on the female. The wing and tail feathers show traces of black, and the beak is red.

Madagascar Lovebird *(Agapornis cana)*

Sometimes known as the Gray-headed Lovebird, the Madagascar Lovebird is not commonly bred, extremely rare, and very expensive. They are smaller than many of the Lovebirds, and like so many of the species are spiteful and high strung. A cock and hen fight so badly that it is wise to keep them apart until they are ready to breed. During incubation, the hen sits on the eggs while the cock attends to her needs.

The head and upper breast of the male are gray, and the rest of the coloring is green. Black marking can be seen on the tail. The female lacks the gray shading of the cock. Her bill is horn-colored, while his is silver. Both sexes have gray feet.

Nyasaland Lovebird (*Agapornis lilianae*)

The Nyasaland Lovebird, or Lilian's Lovebird, comes from Malawi, previously called Nyasaland, and Rhodesia. It is probably the smallest of all the species. Although they are considered free breeders, they are rare in captivity as a result of their characteristic infertility.

The beak is red, and the front of the head, cheeks and throat are orange. The color changes from orange to yellow and on to green at the nape of the neck. This green is carried along the body of the bird. The feet are gray-brown, and the species has a white eye ring.

Black-collared Lovebird (*Agapornis swinderniana*)

The Black-collared Lovebird, or Swindern Lovebird, is found in western Africa and the Congo, but is rarely imported. The birds are green with a blue rump, and a black collar at the back of the neck. The bill is also black.

Suggested Reading

HANDBOOK OF LOVEBIRDS
By Horst Bielfeld
with a special section on
DISEASES OF PARROTS
By Dr. Manfred Heidenreich
ISBN 0-87666-820-1
TFH H-1040

Contents: Lovebirds In The Wild. Keeping Lovebirds. Breeding Lovebirds. Species of Lovebirds: Black-collared, Abyssinian, Red-faced, Gray-headed, Peach-faced, Black-cheeked, Nyasa, Fischer's, Masked. Inheritance Tables. Diseases of Parrots.
Audience: For the aviculturist specializing in lovebirds and owners of parrots of any size. Of interest to novice bird-keepers as well as advanced fanciers.
Hard cover, 8½ x 11", 111 pages, 117 full-color photos, 10 b/w photos.

STARTING RIGHT WITH LOVEBIRDS
By Risa Teitler
ISBN 0-87666-557-1
TFH PS-795

Contents: Introduction. Maintaining a Lovebird. Selecting a Lovebird. Taming and Clipping. First Aid. Breeding Lovebirds.
Hard cover, 8½ x 11", 80 pages
Contains 64 full-color and black and white photos

ALL ABOUT LOVEBIRDS
By P.M. Soderberg
ISBN 0-87666-957-7
TFH PS-742

Contents: Accommodation. Buying Birds. Acclimatization. Water. Feeding. Diseases And Accidents. Lovebirds.
Soft cover, 5½ x 8", 96 pages
17 full-color photos, 29 black and white photos

ALL ABOUT BREEDING LOVEBIRDS
By Mervin F. Roberts
ISBN 0-87666-943-7
TFH PS-800

Contents: Introduction. Species, Hybrids, Varieties. Nutrition. Care and Housing. Breeding. More About Lovebirds. A Technician's View of Handling Birds and Performing Routine Physical Exams
Hard cover, 5½ x 8", 96 pages
Contains over 50 full-color and black and white photos